I0417338

HALSEY

*

*

*

Flying High to Success

*

*

*

Weird and Interesting Facts on
Ashley Nicolette Frangipane!

By Bern Bolo

TABLE OF CONTENTS

***

INTRODUCTION

Okay, so this is yet going to be another introduction for another new artist. As you may have known already, I have been writing quite a number of trivia *(and by that, I meant for the past couple of months…)* I want you guys to sit back and enjoy every page my previous, future and this trivia has to offer. And so without further much blubbering, I'm gonna introduce to you another artist for this trivia and rest assured this is going to be another fun ride!

Of course! Who wouldn't have fun reading about HALSEY right?!!!

Oh yes! You heard that right!

This is going to be about the tattooed girl singer from New Jersey – **HALSEY**!

Get To Know The Tattooed Girl Singer From New Jersey: ASHLEY NICOLETTE FRANGIPANE

Yes, now we have Halsey to blame about the big attention people are giving on pop nowadays. But you see guys... who can blame this talented girl? I mean, she just helped put back the "pop" in POP music.

And because she had been that good with what she does, let us get to know the woman better – better than the tattoos in her body.

So Halsey is born **Ashley Nicolette Frangipane**. She was born on September 29, 1994. She is an American vocalist and lyricist. In 2014, she marked her first recording contract with Astralwerks and discharged her introduction EP, titled "Room 93." She released her first début album on 2015.

In Clark New Jersey is where Halsey was raised. She is the once little girl (and now not so little anymore) of Nicole, who works in a healing facility and Chris Frangipane, who is an auto dealer. She is of Italian, Hungarian, and Irish descent on her mom's side and African-American on her dad's side.

Halsey has two younger siblings namely Sevian and Dante. Growing up, this kid played the violin, viola, and cello until moving onto the acoustic guitar when she was only freaking 14 years old. Halsey initially anticipated heading off to college to major in fine arts, yet she couldn't bear the cost of it, in this way she selected in a junior college as a creative writing major. (*Now, that's a good one Ash...*)

So as I have presented to you just awhile ago, Halsey was constantly keen on music since her youth. In this way at 14 years old, Halsey played the different instruments I have told you about until moving onto the acoustic guitar in 2008.

And also for another fun fact, she is not just good in playing these but she is definitely a decent player of a wide range of musical instruments as well!

Well as for Halsey, she liked music ever since she was a child because she also has grown up with it – I mean she had parents who were both so young at that time!

For Halsey, growing up with an African-American father and a white mother, both parents are still very young, she ended growing up tuning into Biggie, Tupac, Bone Thugs-n-Harmony, her mother was tuning into Nirvana, The Cure, Alanis Morissette and Tori Amos *(and pretty much others in between as well...)*. Like there she was as a young kid and thinking that music is a general dialect and manner in which someone presents strolls of life that are not generally acquainted with individuals.

She experienced childhood in the US and she had this fucking dream-thought of what London resembled as well while tuning into the Arctic Monkeys and fucking whatever else (*if you get what she meant...*), in view of how it was imparted in the tunes. She obviously then has built up her own sentiment of the way life has been for her and yet, she grew up tuning into those two distinct sorts of music and that spoke to a feeling of assorted qualities for her.

So, when she went out into the world, began turning into what she had become now and developing an identity here – then she wasn't very much scared anymore (*as she feared she would be*). There wasn't much that horror (*if that's a better tone to use*) as for her since differing qualities was something that she was utilized to ever since she was a kid. What was only troublesome for her is to be thrown off by something that was different - something that was new.

But as we can obviously see now guys - all in all, Halsey here has played everything cool...

DISCOVERING MUSIC AND BIPOLAR DISEASE

Now first, I am very sorry about the title I hope I did not give you a bad vibe right there but sad to say I just have to stir things around because this is just one of the most important topics there is about our favorite pop singer – Halsey, so let's just get on with it and discuss this sensitive topic, alright?

So I hope you're all up and ready for this…

Anyway, as I have told you, during college days, Halsey began taking up a degree in fine arts and unfortunately for this kid at that time, she was not able to bear the cost of it (*I believe it must be very expensive taking up fine arts at that time…*), so what she did was enrolled herself in a rather lower and cheaper version of the course (*I think…feel free to correct me if I'm wrong here*) and that is Creative writing.

Well for me, I think the course still have something to do with fine arts, right? I mean… *Creative* is being FINE and *Writing* is an ART, so yeah……………

So yeah……………

Yeah…….

I know……….

That was a lame one…………

Anyway! Moving on!

I'm so sorry about the lame and corny jokes dear friend…

I know I promised and have already said that this is a sensitive topic we got here and now I'm cracking these stupidest jokes in the planet! But anyway, I think I made a point there as well right?

But oh fuck! Okay alright…..

Let's move on!

So Halsey definitely had this thing in mind for a long time but unfortunately, she did not have enough bullets to fire off the gun. She experienced money related inconveniences amid her late adolescent years and music turned to be her best option in paying her bills. That is the point at which she began doing appearances in urban areas over the US, under different stage names, "Halsey" turning into the most well-known, one that we know of today!

But before this "inconveniences" in her adolescent years, she already experienced an awful type of inconvenience – *even saying it, is already an inconvenience…*

So during in one specific interview, she boldly said that she has a disease called "*Bipolar Disorder*" and even in her family – it runs (*particularly in her mom*). Well… if ever you have a keen eye and ear, you'll even notice the dual personalities in her songs too like on "*Ghost.*" But yes… when asked about it – she just plainly said that it is, in fact, something she relates to massively and she rarely discusses it in public.

Halsey confessed to having had the illness back when she was only around 16 or 17 years old - but amidst these confessions, nothing still brought this kid down and her singing helped her soothe that monster down too!

A BIT ABOUT THE MONIKER – "*HALSEY*"

So about this… okay so let me get down to this *immediately*, we all know what we call her today, right? It's HALSEY, of course. So as we all know she was born Ashley Nicolette Frangipane but now, we know her better as Halsey. Okay so I'm just going to make this short – I'll explain to you her moniker or professional alias. So her real name is Ashley and actually, the term HALSEY is just the rearranged term from the word *Ashley*…

ASHLEY → HALSEY

See? It's pretty clear and downright straight guys.

It is just an anagram (*an anagram is a formed word by rearranging letters from another word – in case you don't know or just so you know…*) of her name and oh by the way!

Halsey is also a street in Brooklyn where she spent a lot of time as a teenager while growing up – *well….. Where she basically have done shitty and fucked up things, to say the least.*

And so that is it!

CASE CLOSED.

YOUTUBE COVERS & TAYLOR SWIFT

SONGS: *THE TICKET TO THE LIMELIGHT*

So let's start from the beginning on how she discovered that road with a sign "SUCCESS" written on it, okay?

So basically Halsey here started her singing and music profession when she got financially unstable, right? Remember that time in college? Yeah, that one. She knew and had a face-to-face session with music there. That is where she started to like it and love it eventually.

But when she grew more interested in it, she also had done larger measures to get to it like by posting cover songs on YouTube under her genuine name. In 2012, she recorded a spoof of Taylor Swift's "*I Knew You Were Trouble*" song called "*The Haylor Song*" about Swift's association with One Direction member Harry Styles, and posted it on her Tumblr account.

In 2014, Halsey recorded a song called "*Ghost*" and posted it on SoundCloud. The melody picked attention from many viewers and listeners (*especially Swift fans*) under the Astralwerks record label. She then released her introduction EP titled '*Room 93*' on October 27, 2014. Four of the five tunes on the EP contained respective videos.

In 2014, Halsey toured with *The Kooks* as one of their opening acts. At South by Southwest in 2015, Halsey was the most discussed entertainer of the celebration in Twitter. Through March and April 2015, Halsey drove a co-featuring tour with *Young Rising Sons*. She additionally bolstered *Imagine Dragons* on the *Smoke + Mirrors* Tour amid the North American leg on June and August of 2015.

"*BADLANDS*" FOR ALBUM NUMBER ONE!

So "*Badlands*" is the introduction studio album by American vocalist and lyricist Halsey. This had been released on August 28, 2015, by Astralwerks and Capitol Records. The album appeared at number two on the Billboard 200 outline with first-week offers of 97,000 duplicates.

The collection was gone before by the computerized arrival of two singles, "*Ghost*" and "*New Americana*". The third single from the collection, "*Colors*", was out and aired last February 9, 2016.

Another adaptation of the tune "*Castle*" was released as the collection's fourth single to advance the component film, *The Huntsman: Winter's War*. "*Roman Holiday*" was also included in the second period of the TV arrangement Younger and "*I Walk the Line*" was highlighted in the teaser for the film Power Rangers.

As indicated by Halsey, *Badlands* comes from the concept that spotlights on the anecdotal tragic culture known as '*The Badlands*'. The city is encompassed by a deserted wasteland, keeping the occupants of The Badlands hostage.

Halsey states that she made the Badlands as an escape from her own battles in life. As she would see it, the similitude was that even with no escape, there is still positive thinking that there is elsewhere to go.

This collection was officially delivered and produced by Lido. It is an 11-track CD and below is its superb songs:

1. *"Castle"*
2. *"Hold Me Down"*
3. *"New Americana"*
4. *"Drive"*
5. *"Roman Holiday"*
6. *"Colors"*
7. *"Coming Down"*
8. *"Haunting"*
9. *"Control"*
10. *"Young God"*
11. *"Ghost"*

Now I think you may have heard one of these songs already.

Did you like it right?

Oh… no?

You LOVE IT!!!!

"HOPELESS FOUNTAIN KINGDOM" – THE SECOND PROJECT

"*Hopeless Fountain Kingdom*" also adapted as hopeless fountain kingdom is the up and coming second studio collection album by American vocalist Halsey, booked for airing on June 2, 2017, through Astralwerks label.

As for Halsey in a meeting with Rolling Stone last March 2017, *Hopeless Fountain Kingdom* will be an idea collection like her past collection Badlands. The story will fixate on a couple of significant others in a limbo-like domain that associates with the cutting edge setting of the past collection. And since this woman is a MAJOR (*put that in bold*) comic-book kid and lover and a MAJOR Marvel comic geek – this concept is understandable.

On her presentation of the album collection, she said that it was supposed to be a radio collection. Though regardless she considers herself to be an "elective craftsman" she still anticipates that Hopeless Fountain Kingdom will produce some airplay.

Billboard has called attention to that the collection title – saying that it might be named after a genuine fountain made by Halsey's ex-boyfriend off the L train's Halsey Street stop in Brooklyn. (*Well that is sweet…*)

The supposed project is composed of 13 songs, including the single "*Now or Never*."

MISCARRIAGE AND WHAT IT'S LIKE BEING A TROUBLED WOMAN

It's true guys. Everything in this title is just true.

Vocalist Halsey has uncovered that she encountered a miscarriage while touring ahead of her presentation album which had been released a year ago.

The New Jersey local scored achieved Number Two in the US with her introduction collection 'Badlands', released last August 2015, and furthermore hit the outlines with single 'New Americana'. She later showed up on 'The Feeling' from Justin Bieber's collection 'Purpose'.

Addressing Rolling Stone in a sad new interview, Halsey opens up that she got pregnant while on tour last year.

The vocalist reviews what was going through her mind at the time, that she definitely has a lot of things in mind like What happens? Will she lose her record bargain? Will she lose everything? Or, then again will she keep the pregnancy? What are the fans going to think? What are the mothers going to think? What will the Midwest going to think? What's fucking everybody going to think!!!!

Whew….

Well… who could blame her? I mean, pregnancy and having a baby is awesome and is a blessing – but when it comes unexpected and unannounced, you just can't help but be shocked at first, right?

She goes ahead telling that she had a miscarriage in the hotel room that she had been checked in and here's the worse part - she even proceeded to continue the concert that very same fucking day!

Crazy right!!!

Halsey says she "beat herself up" over the unfortunate event. She said that she wasn't drinking. She wasn't doing drugs. She was just fucking exhausted and she felt like her body just simply separated the fuck out!

But amidst all the glory she had experienced in the luxurious lifestyle, she has now, she still made a decision - and that was to be a mom more than anything else - even more than to be a pop star. But unfortunately, everything was too late at that time.

Oh, poor thing… Anyway, still proud of Halsey for her decision to continue the pregnancy though it has already been late for her and for then "future pop star" just like her mom.

Anywho! According to Halsey, these events in her life are heartbreaking that if given to others – they might end up drinking a bottle of Kool-aid and then die. But as for her, she had experienced these unfortunate events even from when she was young. You see, she had been diagnosed with the Bipolar disease, she also admitted to being Bisexual, she is also Biracial (*which she ended up calling herself a "tri-bi"*) and recently, she admitted to being an "inconvenient" woman.

She said, she basically has been living a literal double life ever since, but it was okay with her. Her life was great, her parents (*though young*) had been fine too, her upbringing is great as well. She said that her family understands her and each other which is very good for every child. Her mom especially understands her deeply and loves her and her siblings as well, aside from the fact that her mom is also a bipolar disease victim.

So, see? This wasn't a very good ending at all, is it?

REFERENCES

https://en.wikipedia.org/wiki/Halsey_(singer)

https://en.wikipedia.org/wiki/Halsey_discography

https://en.wikipedia.org/wiki/Badlands_(Halsey_album)

https://en.wikipedia.org/wiki/Hopeless_Fountain_Kingdom

http://www.thefamouspeople.com/profiles/halsey-29890.php

http://frostsnow.com/halsey

http://www.billboard.com/articles/news/6671107/halsey-the-weeknd-drugs-badlands-billboard-feature

http://www.rollingstone.com/music/features/inside-halseys-troubled-past-chaotic-present-w431261

https://www.popjustice.com/articles/halsey-interview-i-dont-believe-people-who-say-theyre-themselves-all-the-time/

http://www.billboard.com/articles/news/cover-story/6971430/billboard-cover-halsey-on-fans-fame-music-success

http://www.nme.com/news/music/halsey-1199540

http://www.fuse.tv/2015/03/new-americana-halsey-sxsw-2015

http://www.imdb.com/name/nm7214498/bio

http://www.billboard.com/artist/6281104/halsey/biography

http://www.kidzworld.com/article/30220-halsey-biography

https://www.youtube.com/user/HalseyVEVO

https://web.facebook.com/HalseyMusic/?_rdc=1&_rdr

https://www.instagram.com/iamhalsey/?hl=en

http://iamhalsey.com/

Racial discrimination? Prejudice? Still rampant! Did you ever wonder what's like to live in the hood? To be judged by the color of your skin or by your nationality? I have heard it's hard, but I never know it firsthand. Kodak had known it all, the harshness of life and the challenges. Did you know that when Black was featured as one of the "2016 Freshman Class" of XXL magazine, his mother upon seeing the issue, was squealing and shouting "Oh My God its Kodak"?! She is indeed a lovely and supportive mother. So, can you let yourself be left behind in the upcoming news? Grab a copy and know all the information about his life, career and challenges. You can also recommend him to your friend who loves rap or who loves music. I know he will be a great inspiration to those who are planning to become one. Well, on the musical aspect of his life can be a great inspiration, the other parts. . . Well, you can just look inside this trivia and decide for yourself.

Check Out KODAK BLACK's Trivia
Get your copy of KODAK BLACK's Trivia!

If you enjoyed this "Trivia", please leave an honest review on Amazon.com!

Sign-up here on Bern Bolo's site for Trivia On Twenty One Pilots!